LEGENDS OF WARFARE

AVIATION

The Huey in Vietnam

Bell's UH-1 at War

DAVID DOYLE

SCHIFFER MILITARY

4880 Lower Valley Road   Atglen, PA 19310

Designed by Justin Watkinson
Type set in Impact/Minion Pro/Univers LT Std

ISBN: 978-0-7643-6275-0
Printed in China

Published by Schiffer Publishing, Ltd.
4880 Lower Valley Road
Atglen, PA 19310
Phone: (610) 593-1777; Fax: (610) 593-2002
E-mail: Info@schifferbooks.com
www.schifferbooks.com

For our complete selection of fine books on this and related subjects, please visit our website at www.schifferbooks.com. You may also write for a free catalog.

Schiffer Publishing's titles are available at special discounts for bulk purchases for sales promotions or premiums. Special editions, including personalized covers, corporate imprints, and excerpts, can be created in large quantities for special needs. For more information, contact the publisher.

We are always looking for people to write books on new and related subjects. If you have an idea for a book, please contact us at proposals@schifferbooks.com.

Acknowledgments

Books of this type are possible only through the combined efforts of many people. This volume was completed with the considerable help of my friends Tom Kailbourn, Jim Gilmore, Dana Bell, Sean Hert, Bob Steinbrunn, Eric Mueller, Scott Taylor, Chris Hughes, and Rich Kolasa. The resources of the National Archives, Army Aviation Museum, National Museum of Naval Aviation, San Diego Air and Space Museum, and Brett Stolle at the National Museum of the United States Air Force provided many of the images. Neither this book nor any of the others could have been completed without the ongoing help and support of my darling wife, Denise.

Contents

Introduction

The Huey is truly one of the icons of the Vietnam War. To the GI, the press, and the public, the ubiquitous helicopter was the Huey, but officially, Bell's versatile creation was the Iroquois, in keeping with US Army policy of naming helicopters after Native American nations.

The Huey was developed in response to a November 1953 Army requirement for a powerful, relatively compact, easily maintained medevac and general-utility helicopter. Twenty firms responded to the invitation to bid, with a contract being awarded to Bell to construct three prototypes of the company's design. Bell called the aircraft the Model 204, and the Army designated it the XH-40. When the XH-40 first flew on October 20, 1956, it heralded the arrival of the era of turboshaft-drive US Army helicopters.

Two additional prototypes followed the first three in 1957, and soon they were joined by six service test, or YH-40, aircraft, the latter of which were actually ordered even before the XH-40 first took to the air.

In March 1960, the Army awarded Bell a production contract for 100 HU-1A, and the nickname "Huey" was born. Even though in September 1962, in accordance with the unified Department of Defense designation system, the aircraft was redesignated the UH-1, the name Huey stuck.

As with many defense systems, the Huey underwent an evolution in design and improvements during the Vietnam era, which are described in the next chapter. The Huey soldiered on after the US withdrawal from Vietnam, including newer and further-improved models. The US Marine Corps UH-1Y "Venom" entered operational service in 2009 and was in production until 2016—a full sixty years from the initial flight of a Huey.

Specifications			
	UH-1B	**UH-1D**	**UH-1N**
Engine make	Lycoming	Lycoming	Pratt & Whitney
Engine model	T53-L-11	T53-L-11	PTCT-3
Horsepower	1,100	1,100	1,100 × 2
Rotor diameter	44 ft.	48 ft.	48 ft., 2¼ in.
Length overall	53 ft.	57 ft., 1 in.	57 ft., 3¼ in.
Length of fuselage	38 ft., 5 in.	41 ft., 6 in.	42 ft., 4¾ in.
Height overall	14 ft., 7 in.	14 ft., 5 in.	14 ft., 5 in.
Empty weight	4,502 lbs.	4,920 lbs.	6,100 lbs.
Loaded weight	9,500 lbs.	9,500 lbs.	10,500 lbs.
Cruising speed	138 mph	125 mph	126 mph
Service ceiling	21,000 ft.	19,390 ft.	17,300 ft.
Hover ceiling IGE	8,200 ft.		12,900 ft.
Hover ceiling OGE	12,500 ft.		4,900 ft.
Range	286 miles	315 miles	248 miles

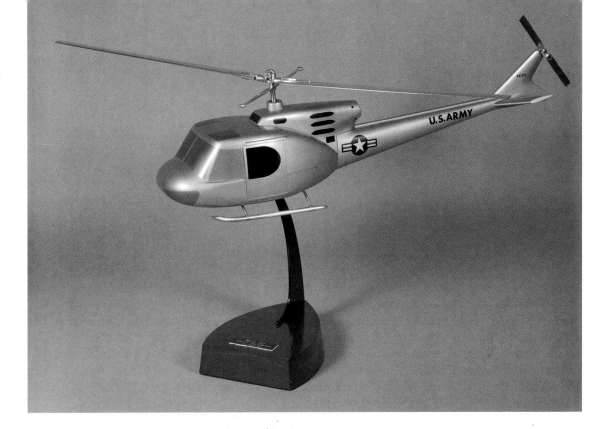

Bell Aircraft produced this conceptual model of an aircraft that would evolve into a series the company designated Model 204, which would be the basis for the UH-1B Iroquois or Huey utility helicopter. The Model 204 was Bell's response to a 1953 US Army requirement for a helicopter to fulfill the roles of general utility, medical evacuation (medevac), and instrument training.

Bell produced this full-sized mockup of a Model 204, which had the US Army designation XH-40. The three operable prototype XH-40s that would be produced served as the first pilots of the Iroquois.

CHAPTER 1
Evolution

While the Army pilots flying the new YH-40 aircraft found them to be a marked improvement over the Army's previous helicopters, these pilots, as was the case with most pilots referring to their aircraft, would have preferred more power. The power plant of the YH-40 and UH-1A was the Lycoming T53-L-1A, delivering a maximum continuous power of 770 shaft horsepower.

In response to the criticism, Bell developed the UH-1B, which flew on the Lycoming T53-L-5, a 960-shaft-horsepower engine. The additional power also allowed an increase in cabin size. The enlarged cabin of the UH-1B could accommodate seven passengers, or, in keeping with the original intent, four stretchers and a medical attendant. Army testing of the UH-1B was initiated in November 1960, and deliveries of production examples began in March 1961.

As the Army began to hang an array of weapons off the sides of the UH-1B, the need for more power arose again, plus aerodynamics were altered. To counter this, the UH-1C was developed. Though initially the UH-1C was powered by the T53L-9 engine, this was quickly superseded by the T53L-11 engine, which delivered 1,100 shaft horsepower. A new, larger rotor blade was developed, which improved maneuverability and, together with the larger engine, provided a slight increase in speed. To counteract the application of this power, a new longer tail boom had to be designed, which included larger synchronized elevators. Fuel capacity was increased to 242 gallons, raising the gross weight to 9,500 pounds, with the payload being almost exactly half of that. Production of the UH-1C began in 1966 and totaled 766 aircraft, ten of which went to overseas customers.

Even before UH-1C production began, work was underway to develop the UH-1D. The UH-1D was an effort to yet again increase the personnel capacity of the aircraft. Bell assembled a full-scale mockup at their plant in Hurst, Texas, which the Army inspected in June 1960. Two weeks later, a contract was issued for seven YUH-1D service test aircraft. The first of these flew on August 16, 1961.

The UH-1D was based on the UH-1B design but featured a fuselage that was 3 feet, 5 inches longer, which combined with rearranged seating meant that fourteen passengers could be carried, or six litters and an attendant. Larger sliding cargo doors, each with two windows, were installed on either side of the passenger area, with a small hinging door adjoining the sliding door, just ahead of it. All of these doors were designed to be readily removable.

Production model UH-1Ds began to be delivered on May 31, 1963. In service, they were dubbed "slicks" because they were not typically fitted with the heavy armament of the UH-1B, instead most often having only M60D door guns. The aircraft featured a 48-foot main rotor with 21-inch cord. To accommodate this, the tail boom was lengthened 18 inches, making the overall length of the UH-1D 41 feet, 6 inches. Production of the type reached 2,561 examples before ceasing in 1966, including 352 built under license by Dornier for the German military.

The UH-1H was an improved model of the UH-1D, featuring the T53L-11 engine generating 1,100 shaft horsepower. Deliveries of the new model began in September 1967, and production reached almost 5,000 of the aircraft, making the UH-1H the mainstay of the Army helicopter force. Beginning in 1969, an improved, crash-resistant fuel system was installed, which reduced fuel capacity to 220 gallons.

By 1965, Bell was experimenting with twin-engine Hueys, starting with the Model 208, basically a modified stretched-fuselage Model 205, with a Continental XT67 twin engine. After the Canadian armed forces ordered fifty of a type designated the CUH-1N Twin Huey (later, CH-135), the US military also placed orders. The US Marine Corps ordered twenty-four, the Navy ordered forty, and the US Air Force ordered seventy-nine of the Twin Hueys, designated UH-1N Iroquois. Additionally, from 1973 through 1978, the Navy and Marines purchased a further 159 examples. The power plant, the PT6T-3/T400 Turbo Twin Pac, contained two Pratt & Whitney Canada PT6 engines driving a single output shaft. The UH-1N could continue to fly on just one PT6 engine.

Initially procured to support missile sites, the UH-1F was built by Bell for the US Air Force. Because the Air Force had a plentiful supply of General Electric T58-GE-3 engines and parts in the supply system, Bell was directed to adapt the Huey to utilize this engine. The result resembles a UH-1B with a UH-1D tail boom. This is because the GE engine developed 1,325 shaft horsepower, requiring a 48-foot rotor, which in turn required the larger tail boom. Because of the difference in engine design, the engine mounting and cowling had to be extensively redesigned.

The aircraft was first flown on February 20, 1964, and deliveries of the 119 production aircraft began in September. Although originally procured for missile site support, the versatile aircraft were soon also being used as staff transport, rescue, and cargo aircraft.

With the increase of US involvement in Vietnam, Air Force UH-1Fs were found in country, initially being used for personnel transport. However, the 20th Special Operations Squadron also used the aircraft in combat roles. Twenty UH-1Fs were modified to become UH-1Ps. Some of these were used in psychological-warfare roles, while others were heavily armed with pintle-mounted GE Miniguns and rocket pods mounted on hardpoints.

As seen in a photo taken along the first XH-40, the Lycoming XT53-L-1 gas-turbine engine served as the power plant for those three prototypes. Rated at 700 shaft horsepower, the XT53-L-1 was an early version of the Lycoming T53 gas-turbine engines that through subsequent upgrades would power various models of UH-1 helicopters.

An XH-40 airframe is under assembly at Bell Aircraft in Hurst, a suburb of Fort Worth, Texas, on August 6, 1956. The instrument panel, with some of the gauges mounted, has been installed in the cockpit, but the engine has yet to be installed.

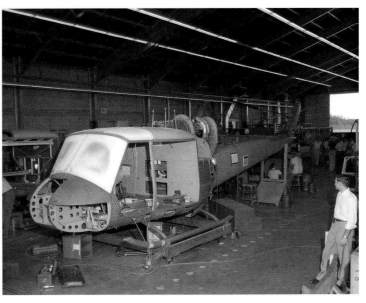

In a photo dated August 6, 1956, the Lycoming XT53-L-1 gas-turbine engine has been installed in the upper rear of the fuselage (the part of the airframe from the nose to the front of the tail boom) of the first Bell XH-40. Prominent, vertical frame members with numerous lightening holes were on the inner sides of cutouts for curved chin windows.

The first XH-40 is pictured as completed. The serial number 55-4459 is on the tail boom. Except for the dome-shaped fairing and engine air-intake scoops over the transmission, the helicopter had the overall appearance of production UH-1s to come. The access cover has been removed at the joint of the tail boom and the vertical fin (also called the tail pylon) to expose the intermediate gearbox of the tail rotor driveshafts. On the left side of the nose is a pitot tube.

The fairings for the transmission, engine, and tail-rotor shafts of one of the XH-40 prototypes have been removed for this test hover at the Bell plant, and no stabilizer bar is present below the main rotor. The exhaust nozzle is prominent on the rear of the Lycoming XT53-L-1 engine. Projecting from the rear of the tail boom is the tail skid, meant to protect the tail rotor should the tail swing too close to the ground.

By the time this photo of the first XH-40, serial number 55-4459, was taken, fins had been added to the outer ends of the elevators. A pitot tube was on the left side of the nose. This aircraft first flew on October 20, 1956, with Bell Aircraft's chief pilot, Floyd W. Carlson, and chief experimental test pilot Elton J. Smith at the controls.

Bell XH-40 prototype number 2, serial number 55-4460, exhibited several differences from the first prototype XH-40. A test-equipment pod was mounted above the main rotors. Two vertical FM homing antennas were on stub mounts on the nose, and the elevators had been moved forward on the tail boom. All three XH-40s have diagonally arranged louver vents on the lower rears of the cabin doors, which were of sliding design.

The third XH-40 is marked with the number 3; tail number 54461, representing serial number 55-4461; and "ARMY" on the vertical fin. "BELL Helicopter CORP.," with "Helicopter" in script, and "XH-40" are marked on the aft part of the cabin. The stabilizer bar on this prototype was above the main rotors, and counterweights were added below the outer sides of the semirigid rotor head.

Bell XH-40 prototype number 3 is resting on a rain-saturated area at an unidentified airbase. Unlike prototypes 1 and 2, this helicopter lacked the air-intake scoops on the aft part of the transmission fairing; instead, the fairing had a large opening in that area, with a fore-and-aft frame member at the top.

At the same airfield, technicians are checking out the third prototype XH-40. Two arch-shaped recessed steps are on the side of the cabin aft of the cabin door. Faintly visible is a long spline on the top of the cabin, with red, white, and blue stripes on it.

Bell Aircraft manufactured six YH-40 service-test helicopters, with the Army's order for these aircraft being tendered before the first flight of the XH-40. Notable changes to the exterior included a lower transmission fairing and a revamped engine air-intake scoop and engine fairing. Two scoop vents were added to the top of the cockpit. Less noticeable was the fact that the overall length of the airframe was increased by 1 foot. The engine for the YH-40s was the Lycoming T53-L-1A.

The first YH-40 bears the tail number 66723, which related to serial number 56-6723. Counterweights were mounted under the semirigid rotor head. Detachable ground-handling wheels are on the landing skids. A new feature was the fairing on the upper rear of the engine fairing, to hold a UHF antenna and an anticollision light.

The HU-1A (redesignated UH-1A in 1962) was the first production model of the US Army's Iroquois helicopters. As may be seen in this example, serial number 58-3017, marked with high-visibility orange paint to indicate its status as a trainer, the HU-1A resembled the service-test YH-40. The photograph was taken at Shell Army Heliport, Fort Rucker, Alabama.

Bell HU-1B, serial number 60-3589, is armed with two M3 launchers for 2.75-inch folding-fin aerial rockets (FFAR). The airframe of the HU-1B was 31 inches longer than that of the HU-1A, to allow more room for seating and carrying stretchers. The HU-1B (redesignated UH-1B in 1962) differed from the HU-1A in appearance principally in the visibly taller main-rotor mast. The Lycoming T53-L-5 turbine engine was used in this model.

Early on in the HU-1A's service, examples were used as test beds for air-to-ground rocket and missile systems. This HU-1A with high-visibility orange markings is equipped with the M22 Armament Subsystem, featuring launch racks on each side with three AGM-22 wire-guided antitank missiles.

UH-1B, serial number 63-12923, continues to fly under civil registration number N370AS and was refinished in US Navy markings. In this photo, the left external-stores support is armed with a Minigun and a seven-tube M158 launcher for 2.75-inch rockets, and a flexible machine gun is mounted in the door. A blade antenna was retrofitted on the cockpit roof, and at some point a particle filter was installed over the engine-air intake. *Rich Kolasa*

On the right side of the same UH-1B are M158 rocket-launcher tubes and a flexible-mounted M2 HB .50-caliber machine gun (the rider has his hand on the barrel) and ammo box. The fuel filler is visible through the window of the cabin door. *Rich Kolasa*

The US Army Aviation Museum, Fort Rucker, Alabama, preserves Bell UH-1B, serial number 60-3554. Installed on the right external-stores support are an M158 rocket launcher and the Armament Subsystem M6, consisting of two M60C 7.62 mm machine guns along with their mounts, flexible ammunition chutes, and ammunition boxes in the rear of the cabin, below the red canvas seats.

The Armament Subsystem M6 allowed for the copilot to sight and control the M60C machine guns, elevating them from +9 degrees to –66 degrees from horizontal, and traversing them from 12 degrees inboard to 70 degrees inboard, with fire interrupted should the guns be pointed at the airframe. Hydraulic lines were provided for powering the elevation and traverse of the guns. Inside the cabin is a rear-facing seat.

The M158 rocket launcher and the twin M60C 7.62 mm machine guns on the right side of UH-1B, serial number 60-3554, are viewed from the front. Attached to the external-stores support, the curved structure next to the cabin, is the gun mount, on the outer end of which are the two machine guns. On the front face of the gun mount are two cartridge drives for the ammunition chutes.

The data stencil on the side of the cabin aft of the copilot's door provides the helicopter's nomenclature (UH-1B), its serial number (60-3554), and fuel specifications. In view in the cabin are red canvas crew seats and 7.62 mm ammunition boxes.

Nicknamed the "Huey Hog," the UH-1C was designed from the start as a gunship / transport helicopter pending production of the AH-1G Huey Cobra gunship. The Lycoming T53-L-9 or -11 engine, more powerful than the engine in the UH-1B, permitted the UH-1C to bear the weight of weapons systems, which included the M75 40 mm grenade launcher in a nose turret, and various gun pod, rocket, and missile combinations. Other improvements to the UH-1C included larger elevators and wide-chord Bell model 540 main rotors, with a much more substantial rotor head than on the UH-1B. This example, the second UH-1C produced by Bell, serial number 64-14102, was armed with M3 2.75-inch FFAR launchers.

Looks can be deceiving: at first glance—this would appear to be a UH-1C, but the narrow-chord rotor blades, the pitot tube on the nose, and the presence of the fuel filler on the right rear of the cabin are clues that this is a UH-1B, specifically a Huey Hog trainer.

Bell completed a total of seven YHU-1D service-test helicopters, precursors of the UH-1D, with the first flight occurring in August 1961. As seen in a photo of YHU-1D, serial number 60-6028, this model had a stretched cabin, 3 feet, 5 inches longer than the cabin of the -B model, with a cabin door with two windows and a narrow door, which the technical manuals referred to as a hinged doorpost panel, with an optional single window on each side. The longer cabin enabled the helicopter to carry up to fifteen persons, including the crew. With this personnel capacity, the UH-1D saw service primarily as a troop carrier.

In a view of the right side of YHU-1D, serial number 60-6028, the fuel filler is visible on the fuselage aft of the cabin door. These helicopters were powered by the Lycoming T53-L-9 engine.

The first deliveries of the UH-1D (Bell model 205) to the US Army were in August 1963. Shown here is UH-1D, serial number 65-9738. The antitorque pedals, also called yaw-control pedals, are visible through the chin window. The large blade antenna on the cockpit roof is the VHF. The grab-bar-shaped device farther aft on the roof is VHF/UHF homing antenna number 1, sometimes called the "towel rack antenna." Adjoining the front of the cabin door is what in official nomenclature is a hinged doorpost panel, with a window. Bell UH-1Ds were equipped with the T-53-L-11 engine and, later in production, the T-53-L-13 engine.

The US Navy was a user of the UH-1D, such as Bureau Number (BuNo) 659739, from Antarctic Development Squadron 6 (VXE-6) during a flight from Naval Air Station Quonset Point, Rhode Island, in 1969.

The Bell UH-1E was a US Marine Corps assault-support version of the Huey, thirty-four of which were based on UH-1B airframes and 158 of which were based on UH-1Cs. It featured a rescue hoist on the right side of the cabin roof, USMC communications gear, a brake for immobilizing the main rotor during operations on ships, and all-aluminum construction, to combat corrosion. The Marines received their first UH-1Es in late February 1964. This UH-1E is BuNo 151267. Protruding from the tail boom are posts for a high-frequency wire antenna.

The zigzag shape of a high-frequency antenna is visible along the tail boom of UH-1E, BuNo 155349, tail code 27, assigned to Marine Light Helicopter Squadron 267 (HML-267) "Ace of Spades," at Naval Air Facility China Lake, California, in May 1977. The raised device on the engine fairing is an engine air-intake particle filter.

The UF-1F was a US Air Force version of the Huey, tasked with flying personnel and cargo to intercontinental ballistic missile sites. The Air Force drew on its surplus stock of General Electric T-58-GE-3 engines to power the UF-1Fs, and a new fairing was developed to cover those power plants and to route the exhaust nozzle to the right instead of the rear. Shown in flight is US Air Force serial number 65-7940, one of 119 UH-1Fs delivered from 1964 to 1967.

Bell UF-1F, serial number 65-7922 and construction number 7063, was added to the collections of the National Museum of the United States Air Force in 2003. This helicopter served at Francis E. Warren Air Force Base, Wyoming, and in 1984 was transferred to Sheppard Air Force Base, Texas, where, redesignated as a GUH-1F, it served as a ground instructional airframe. The door on the engine nacelle, hinged on the rear, is open.

Mounted on the final-drive right-angle gearbox of the GUH-1F, the tail rotor is formed of laminated fiberglass over a honeycomb core. The insignia of the Air Education and Training Command is on the tail pylon. Toward the rear of the tail boom are the left omnidirectional VHF navigation antenna, resembling a grab handle, and a red position light.

With the fairing of the GUH-1F open, the General Electric T-58-GE-3 engine is visible. Output from the engine is transmitted forward to the transmission (above the cabin door), which directs output up to the main rotor.

Above the transmission are the swash plate, the main-rotor mast, the main rotor assembly, and, at the top, the stabilizer bar. To the lower left is the oil tank, with a yellow filler cap. Above that cap is the engine-intake guard, formed from mesh screen and a brownish frame.

The cockpit of the GUH-1F at the National Museum of the United States Air Force is viewed through the left door. The pilot sat in the right seat, and the copilot in the left. The seats are the conventional type—that is, not the armored model—with red upholstery. To the lower left is the copilot's collective pitch-control lever; to the front of the seat are the cyclic control stick and the antitorque pedals, with the Bell logo on them. A black antiglare hood is over the instrument panel.

The pilot's seat and cyclic and collective controls are viewed through the right door. The console between the pilots' seats was referred to as the pedestal panel. On the pilot's side of the console is a small circuit-breaker panel.

The asymmetrical positioning and layout of the instrument panel is evident, with the bulk of the instruments weighted toward the pilot's side. Above the pedestal panel are the fuel gauge, oil-pressure indicators, and two voltmeters. The box on the top of the pilot's collective pitch-control lever, to the right of the pedestal, includes switches for the starter, governor rpm, engine-idle stop release, and landing light / searchlight. On the collective lever below that switch box is the pilot's twist-grip throttle control.

The rotor-brake control, the overhead console, and quilted sound-deadening material on the ceiling are viewed from the pilot's position looking to the left. Aft of the rotor-brake control is a utility light with a coiled power cord.

As seen through the left cockpit door, the center of the ceiling of the GUH-1F cockpit, between the overhead windows is the overhead console, with switch and circuit breaker panels for various electrical systems. On the far side of the console is the main-rotor brake lever, for immediately stopping the rotation of the rotor after the engine is shut down.

The forward approximately two-thirds of the overhead console is devoted to electrical switches and controls, while the rear contains circuit breakers. Green tinting for the copilot's overhead window is in the background.

Details of the pilots' seats and flight controls are displayed. The lever on the side of each seat is for locking and unlocking the harness. The unarmored seats were adjustable for height and fore-and-aft position but not for reclining. A data plate is on the doorjamb to the right.

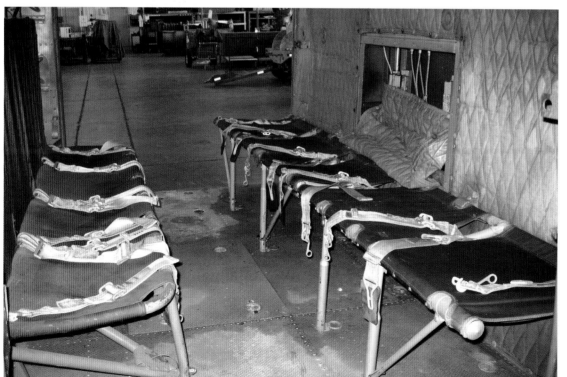

Personnel seats in the GUH-1F, as viewed through the left cabin door, are of reinforced canvas on tubular frames. The forward seats (*left*) are red and have canvas seat backs, while the rear seats are Olive Drab. Lap safety belts are provided.

The model of the Huey produced in the greatest numbers was the UH-1H. Essentially, the UH-1H was similar to the UH-1D but with a more powerful engine, the Lycoming T53-L-13. Nicknamed the "Hotel" because of the model's "H" suffix, these helicopters also had on the cockpit roof an L-shaped pitot tube and a VHF blade antenna. Some UH-1Hs were built as such, while numbers of UH-1Ds were converted to -H standards by installing the T53-L-13 engine and making other revisions. This UH-1H at Wiesbaden Air Base, West Germany, has a wire-strike kit on the cockpit roof and under the cockpit, for cutting a highline should the helicopter accidentally fly into one.

An example of a still-flying UH-1H is serial number 66-16101, with civil registration number N661TX, owned by Air Cav Helicopters LLC, Wilmington, Delaware. The helicopter is equipped with a wire-strike kit above and below the cockpit. *Rich Kolasa*

Army Aviation Heritage Foundation, Inc., of Hampton, Georgia, preserves UH-1H, serial number 70-16426 and civil registration number N426HF. Atop the tail pylon is a whip antenna for an FM radio. The two small, arched fairings on the nose are for the AN/APR-39 radar-warning receiver, and the slanted antenna on the cockpit roof is FM communications antenna number 2. Two covers for recessed steps are on the column between the pilot's door and the cabin door, with black stripes above them. *Rich Kolasa*

A restored UH-1H has markings on the nose for the Experimental Military Unit (EMU), a company-sized helicopter assault force composed of personnel from the US Army and the Fleet Air Arm of the Royal Australian Navy (RAN). The EMU served in the Vietnam War from 1967 to 1971. *Chris Hughes*

A reenactor door gunner is manning an M60 7.62 mm machine gun in the same UH-1H with EMU markings. The cover for the tail rotor driveshaft on the tail pylon is in bare-metal finish. *Chris Hughes*

The EMU-marked UH-1H approaches the camera. The EMU insignia on the nose features a union shield with wings and anchor, with these inscriptions: "USA RAN" (*top*), "EMU" (*below center*), and "GET THE BLOODY JOB DONE" (*bottom*). *Chris Hughes*

In a head-on shot of a UH-1H in a hover just above the ground, a small, black stencil on the center of the nose reads "BATTERY ACCESS" over "RADIO ACCESS." These refer to a large access panel between the chin windows, extending up almost to the windshield. *Rich Kolasa*

Bell UH-1H, serial number 68-16309 and civil registration number N911JM, has been restored and bears US Army markings. The engine access panel is open, as is the side panel on the aft part of the fuselage. The hinged doorpost panel, to the rear of the copilot's door, lacks the optional single window.
Chris Hughes

The left engine access panel and hold-open brace of the UH-1H are seen close-up, along with the Lycoming T53-L-13 turboshaft engine, rated at 1,400 shaft horsepower. Atop the engine fairing to the far right is the red anticollision light. *Chris Hughes*

The right cabin door of the UH-1H is shown fully open. These doors were fabricated from aluminum skin on aluminum frames, with clear plastic windows. The placard behind the windows that reads "EXPERIMENTAL" refers to the Federal Aviation Administration's "Experimental" classification, which, among other things, applies to aircraft used in flight exhibitions. *Chris Hughes*

The right sides of the fairings for the engine and transmission are in view, along with the engine exhaust nozzle, the anticollision light, and the main rotor and its mast. Elements of the engine are visible behind the ventilation screens on the side of the fairing. *Chris Hughes*

The interior of the cabin of the UH-1H is covered with quilted insulation material. The insulated ceiling and bulkhead of the cabin is shown in detail. The troop seats could be removed readily, to permit carrying cargo. *Chris Hughes*

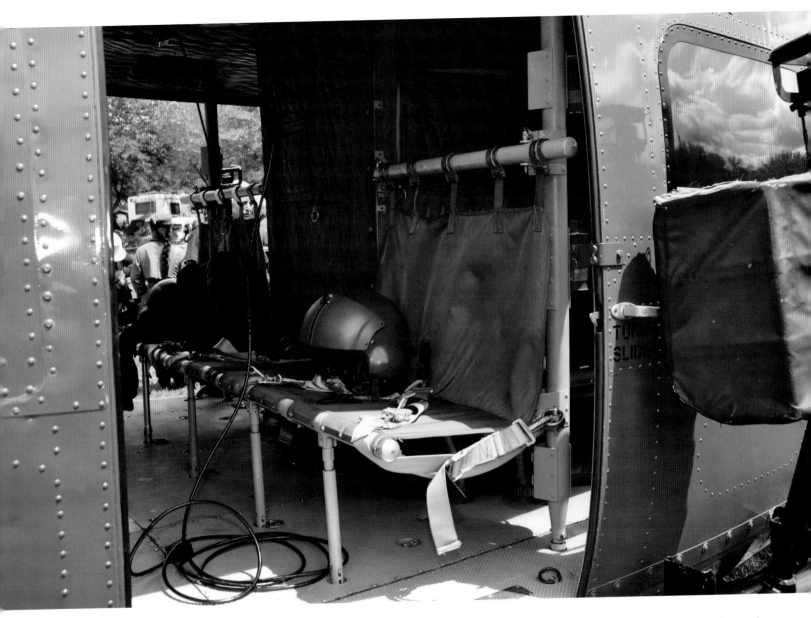

Troop seats in the cabin of the UH-1H consist of canvas seats and backs strapped to tubular frames. Lap safety belts are provided. An aircrew helmet is resting on the seat. *Chris Hughes*

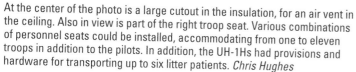

At the center of the photo is a large cutout in the insulation, for an air vent in the ceiling. Also in view is part of the right troop seat. Various combinations of personnel seats could be installed, accommodating from one to eleven troops in addition to the pilots. In addition, the UH-1Hs had provisions and hardware for transporting up to six litter patients. *Chris Hughes*

An Armament Subsystem M23 is installed on this UH-1H, consisting of an M60D 7.62 mm machine gun on a pintle mount, on a pedestal mounted on an external-stores support. The M60D is equipped with two handgrips; a folding bipod is on the muzzle end of the barrel. A spent-casing bag is next to the receiver of the gun. *Chris Hughes*

The left Armament Subsystem M23 on a UH-1H is viewed from the rear. The two features jutting up from the cylindrical base of the unit are holders for a 7.62 mm ammunition box. In actual use, a flexible ammo chute would be connected to the ammunition box and the left side of the machine gun. *Chris Hughes*

Two members of the Iroquois/Huey family make an appearance together: a Bell AH-1 Cobra gunship and a UH-1H. The Cobra enjoyed a successful career with the US Army for over thirty years before being superseded by the AH-64 Apache and retired from US Army service in 2001. *Rich Kolasa*

USMC UH-1N, BuNo158260, shows off the lines of the UH-1N: the nose was slightly lengthened and made less blunt, the size of the chin windows was reduced, and the engine and transmission fairings were completely redesigned. *National Museum of Naval Aviation*

During the Vietnam War the US Air Force converted a small number of its UH-1F helicopters to UH-1Ps, for use by special-operations units, particularly the 20th Special Operations Squadron. Reportedly, these helicopters were equipped as gunships, carrying Miniguns and rockets. Like the UH-1F, the UH-1P had two tandem antennas on the cabin roof, and its engine exhaust nozzle was pointed to the right. Here, a UH-1P fitted out for medevac service is taking off from MacDill Air Force Base, Florida, during a training exercise.

The National Museum of the US Air Force preserves this UH-1P, serial number 65-7925. It was built as a UH-1F and delivered to the US Air Force in March 1966, serving briefly with the 43rd Bombardment Wing at Little Rock Air Force Base, Arkansas, before being transferred to the 606th Air Commando Squadron at Nakhon Phanom Royal Thai Air Force Base in July 1966. The helicopter was transferred to the 20th Special Operations Squadron at Nha Tran Air Base, Republic of Vietnam, in February 1967, and in June 1969 it was converted to a UH-1P gunship. After November 1970, it served with several training and rescue units; it was retired from service in late 1987 and was transferred to the Museum of the US Air Force in 1992.

UH-1P, serial number 65-7925, is on static display in the National Museum of the US Air Force. A swiveling pedestal mount for an M60 7.62 mm machine gun has been mounted inside the door.

In addition to the right-facing engine-exhaust nozzle, a recognition feature of the UH-1P was the short, UH-1B-style cabin with the long, UH-1D-style tail boom. The long tail boom was necessitated by the larger-diameter main rotor.

The UH-1P has been painted in a Southeast Asia camouflage scheme, with tan and two shades of green over gray. Quilted sound-insulation material is on the rear bulkhead of the cabin. On the left side of the nose is the pitot tube. An access door is toward the forward end of the tail boom.

A 7.62 mm Minigun is installed on a flexible, gunner-operated mount in the right door. This rotary-barrel, electrically operated gun could fire at a rate of up to 6,000 rounds per minute without overheating. The US Air Force designated this weapon the GAU-2B/A, while the Army's designation is M134. This UH-1P, displayed at the Museum of Aviation at Robins Air Force Base, Georgia, has markings on the pilot's door commemorating Darwin Edwards, who was the curator of that museum. He flew this very helicopter while assigned to the 20th Special Operations Squadron in the Vietnam War and played a key role in acquiring it for the museum.

The GAU-2B/A Minigun is viewed from its left side. It is mounted in a cradle, which pivots on a pintle mount that is incorporated into a heavy-duty base, which is bolted to the floor. Two pistol grips are on the rear of the cradle.

A flexible feed chute is routed from the Minigun to the top of a 7.62 mm ammunition magazine in the rear of the cabin.

The Minigun cradle (*left*) has a ring and bead sight on top of it. The left handgrip is behind the cradle. At the bottom center is the base for the Minigun mount; in the center background is the 7.62 mm ammunition magazine.

Above the transmission fairing of the UH-1P are, *from the bottom up*, the swash plate, the main rotor mast (flanked by the two blade-pitch control rods), the rotor head and rotor blades, and the stabilizer bar.

Details of the engine and transmission fairings, the swash plate and lower part of the main rotor mast, and the cabin roof are displayed. To the right is the aft blade antenna. On the roof at the center of the photo is the upper-right position light, with a green lens (the upper position light on the left side has a red lens). Inboard and aft of the upper-right position light is another position light with a clear lens.

The exhaust nozzle of the General Electric T-58-GE-3 turboshaft engine protrudes from the right rear of the engine fairing of the UH-1P. Also in view are a panel with louvered vents aft of the cabin door, and an access door on the tail boom.

Details are presented for the windshield frame, windshield wipers, roof vent scoops, and antennas of the UH-1P at the Museum of Aviation, at Robins Air Force Base. Boxes for 7.62 mm ammunition are in the center rear of the cabin.

A view through the pilot's door of the UH-1P at the Museum of Aviation takes in the instrument panel, pedestal, and collective and cyclic controls. On the underside of the antiglare hood over the instrument panel are four secondary lights, for illuminating the instrument panel.

The pedestal panel between the pilot's and copilot's seats contains controls for various systems, including the radios.

From a different angle through the pilot's door of the UH-1P, the overhead console is in view at the top. Details of the copilot's seat and door and the yellow emergency-exit markings above and to the front of the door are in view.

A view through the right cabin door takes in the rears of the pilots' seats, the pedestal panel, and the overhead console and windows.

CHAPTER 2

In Vietnam

The Huey arrived in Vietnam in March 1962, when aircraft of the 57th Medical Detachment arrived. As the number of Hueys in country increased, so did their roles. The UH-1B and UH-1C models were used as gunships, a role in which, beginning in 1967, they were largely supplanted by a more specialized helicopter, the AH-1 Cobra.

The Huey did yeoman work in Vietnam, delivering men and supplies and, arguably even more importantly, extracting troops and wounded, often under withering enemy fire. It is no surprise that out of 7,013 Hueys sent to Vietnam, 3,305 were destroyed, and, more tragically, 1,074 Huey pilots and 1,103 other Huey crew members were killed.

The Huey was also the aircraft of extraordinary heroism, with six Army, one Air Force, and one Marine Huey crewmen receiving the Medal of Honor for in-flight actions, and three more for heroism when not in flight.

Armed with eight-pack 2.75-inch FFARs and a .30-caliber M1919 machine gun on fixed mounts, a UH-1A flies ground support over South Vietnam on February 21, 1963. This US Army Huey, serial number 59-1695, was probably assigned to the UTT Helicopter Company. *National Archives*

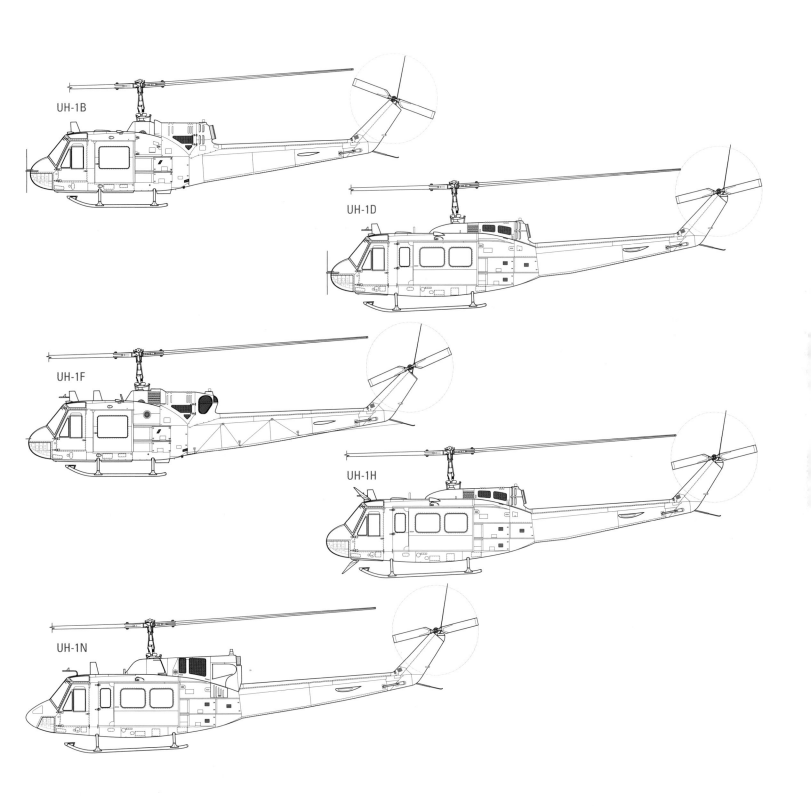

UH-1B

UH-1D

UH-1F

UH-1H

UH-1N

Utility Tactical Transport (UTT) Helicopter Company Specialists Johnson and Kelson conduct maintenance on a UH-1B's generator at Tân Sơn Nhứt Air Base, Saigon, on February 21, 1963. The oil tank, with its blue oil-line connections and yellow filler cap, can be seen to the right of Specialist Kelson's knee. *National Archives*

Based at Tân Sơn Nhứt Air Base in Saigon, Republic of Vietnam, Specialists Gordon Johnson and Almer Kelson sight in an eight-pack 2.75-inch FFAR multiple launcher on a UH-1B helicopter on February 21, 1963. Specialists Johnson and Kelson served with the UTT Company at the airbase. *National Archives*

Specialist 5 Joseph McGurk slips a 2.75-inch folding-fin aerial rocket into an eight-pack launch tube, while an adjustment is made by Specialist 4 Weldon Reynolds, in the rear. Both men are at work in the UTT Helicopter Company area at Saigon's Tân Sơn Nhứt Air Base, on February 21, 1963. *National Archives*

At Saigon's Tân Sơn Nhứt Airbase on February 21, 1963, Glenn Martin, a specialist 4th class of the UTT Helicopter Company, is loading a .30-caliber Browning M1919 machine gun. The weapon is fitted into an improvised mount on a UH-1A helicopter. Inside the cargo compartment is a large ammunition box, the ammo belt from which has been routed to the machine gun through openings in the floor and fuselage of the aircraft. *National Archives*

At a base in South Vietnam on September 25, 1964, two of the war's workhorses await their next mission: a US Army UH-1B Iroquois helicopter and a US Air Force Douglas A-1E Skyraider. On the nose of the UH-1B is an insignia featuring a white eagle with the number 6. *National Archives*

Perhaps the same helicopter as in the preceding photo, a UH-1B, and a Republic of Vietnam Air Force Douglas A-1E Skyraider soar over a delta area in the Southeast Asian country. The Huey's nose and the rear of its cabin feature the white eagle insignia. *National Archives*

Arrayed in lines on the amphibious assault ship USS *Iwo Jima* (LPH-2) are Bell UH-1D helicopters. A cameraman perched atop the crates to the left films the aircraft taking off for their land bases as *Iwo Jima* steams off the coast of Vietnam on April 12, 1965. *National Archives*

Having leaped out of a UH-1B during a mission in Vietnam on September 12, 1965, Sgt. Dennis Troxel is priming the M60C machine guns. Troxel was a member of the 25th Infantry Division but served as a volunteer "shotgun rider" aboard this 179th Aviation Company Huey. *National Archives*

UH-1D Hueys get ready to airlift members of the 2nd Battalion, 14th Infantry Regiment, out of the Filhol Rubber Plantation to a new staging area. Operation Wahiawa was underway, a search-and-destroy mission in the area northeast of Cù Chi in the Republic of Vietnam. *National Archives*

Medical evacuation—medevac—became an iconic UH-1 mission in the Vietnam conflict. Here, a UH-1D picks up a casualty in Hậu Nghĩa Province on May 21, 1966, during the 25th Infantry Division's search-and-destroy mission known as Operation Wahiawa. *National Archives*

On a base in Vietnam, US Army UH-1B Hueys are receiving maintenance on May 18, 1966. There are areas painted orange on the upper rear parts of the helicopter cabins. Sitting between the choppers is a service cart loaded with a tank for fuel or oil. A tricycle service car can be seen to the right. *National Archives*

A UH-1B Huey ferries supplies to the radio relay station Camp Dean, located on Black Virgin Mountain (Núi Bà Đen) in Tây Ninh Province, northwest of Saigon near the Cambodian border in early June 1966. On top of a large rock to the left is a bunker protected by sandbags and decorated with the camp builders' graffiti. *National Archives*

In the course of Operation Fort Smith in early June 1966, UH-1 Hueys transport elements of the 25th Infantry Division in Ap An Bien, near Cù Chi, northwest of Saigon, where the division's base camp was located. A door-mounted M60 machine gun's barrel is visible in the foreground. *National Archives*

Swooping low over rice paddies with its sliding door open and its auxiliary door removed, a UH-1D takes part in Operation Fort Smith. A silhouette of a white bear is visible on the rear of the sliding door in this companion photo to the preceding 1966 image. Also noteworthy is the yellow-painted tail skid on this Huey. *National Archives*

During the Vietnam War, Huey helicopters regularly airlifted supplies wherever they were needed, operating as some sort of flying cargo trucks or jeeps. Here, on July 31, 1966, the cabin of a UH-1D is loaded with boxes of C rations by troops of the 3rd Brigade, 25th Infantry Division. *National Archives*

Men of the 4th Battalion, 503rd Infantry, 173rd Airborne Brigade, pour out of a UH-1D that has landed at the brigade's forward base in Xuân Lộc, east of Saigon, in the Republic of Vietnam. The date is September 1, 1966, and the troops have just successfully concluded a search-and-destroy mission. *National Archives*

Operation Kamuala was conducted by the 2nd Battalion, 14th Infantry, 25th Infantry Division, with the aim of interdicting food supplies to enemy forces. Here, on September 27, 1966, a suspected Việt Cộng family is led to UH-1D, serial number 65-9608, for evacuation. *National Archives*

Nicknamed the "Hotel," the UH-1H was the Huey version that was manufactured in the greatest numbers. Although many UH-1H choppers were built in that configuration, a number of UH-1Ds were converted to UH-1H standards. The conversion involved various modifications, including the installation of the Lycoming T53-L-13 turbine engine, with 1,400 shaft horsepower. Other conversion changes included moving the pitot tube from the nose's left side to the roof of the cockpit, and installing a "towel bar" FM antenna in front of the transmission on the roof. The first flight of a YUH-1H service-test prototype took place in 1966, and production UH-1Hs began to be delivered in September 1967. By 1982, the US Army alone had received about 5,000 of the helicopters. Over subsequent decades, improvements were constantly made to the chopper to keep it competent. Under license, Germany, Japan, Italy, and Taiwan have built UH-1Hs. The example that appears in this image served with the Republic of Vietnam Air Force in 1971. *National Archives*

Troops of the 4th Battalion, 503rd Infantry, are airlifted aboard a UH-1D to the forward base camp of the 173rd Airborne Brigade in Xuân Lộc District, Long Khánh Province, east of Saigon, Republic of Vietnam, following a successful September 1, 1966, search-and-destroy mission. *National Archives*

This UH-1B crashed while on a test flight around Sóc Trăng in the Mekong River delta south of Saigon on October 2, 1966. The Huey, which served with the 336th Aviation Company, 13th Aviation Battalion, 1st Aviation Brigade, is here displaying its avionics equipment thanks to the absence of its nose enclosure. *National Archives*

One UH-1D takes to the air on a mission against the Việt Cộng while men of Company C, 503rd Airborne Infantry, await pickup by another Huey. The US forces are taking part in Operation Meridian, a search-and-destroy operation in an area about 46 miles northwest of Biên Hòa on November 10, 1966. *National Archives*

Four UH-1D Hueys in camouflage paint come in to land as the men of Company B, 2nd Battalion, 503rd Airborne Infantry, 173rd Airborne Brigade (Separate), move forward through an open area in the course of Operation Meridian on November 10, 1966. *National Archives*

A Huey is being repaired on the deck of USNS *Corpus Christi Bay*, a floating aircraft maintenance depot that was anchored in Cam Ranh Bay on November 12, 1966. The ship's maintenance area boasted large cranes that could lift engines and other large or heavy parts, such as the chopper's rotor, which here has been hoisted above the rotor mast. *Corpus Christi Bay's* marked-off helipad can be seen in the foreground. *National Archives*

Bell Helicopter's UH-1 could be adapted to various roles as communications and command helicopters. Seen here at Landing Zone Hammond, Republic of Vietnam, on February 9, 1967, is an AN/ARC-122 communication center installed aboard a UH-1B. An RT-246 VHF low-band radio set is also a part of this installation. *National Archives*

A search-and-destroy mission begins with a Civilian Irregular Defense Group (CIDG) member jumping from a UH-1D northwest of Tuy Hòa on November 23, 1966. Installed on an M23 mount aboard the aircraft is an M60D 7.62 mm machine gun. *National Archives*

Armed with quad 7.62 mm machine guns and seven-shot 2.75-inch FFAR pods, this US Navy UH-1B Huey is serving with Attack Squadron (Light) 3 "Seawolves" at Vĩnh Long on January 12, 1967. UH-1 helicopters belonging to the Navy provided assistance to riverine patrol craft whose job was to interdict Việt Cộng activity on waterways. *National Museum of Naval Aviation*

A CH-47 Chinook has airlifted this UH-1B, with the markings "Maverick" and "36" visible on the cabin, to Tân Sơn Nhứt Air Base's heliport in Saigon in February 1967. The Huey will then be shipped to the United States for renovation. *National Archives*

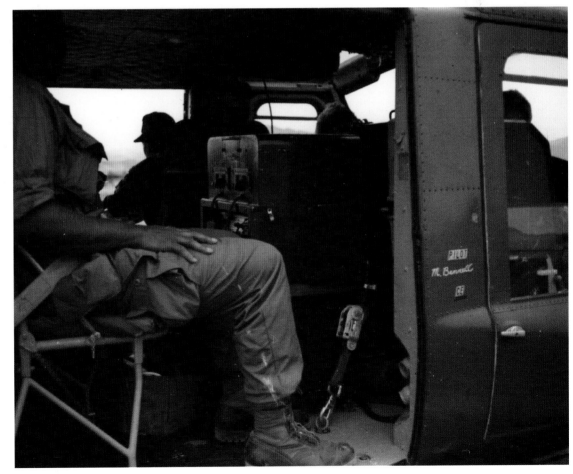

At a base in Vietnam, an AN/ASC-6 airborne command radio is being fitted into the cabin of a Bell UH-1B Iroquois. The helicopter in this May 25, 1967, photo has "PILOT / M. Bennett" marked toward the right on the door. *National Archives*

While hovering over the ground in Bình Định Province, a UH-1D drops supplies to Company D, 1st Battalion, 7th Cavalry, during Operation Pershing, a search-and-destroy mission. Dropping supplies in this manner was called "low-level kickoff." *National Archives*

This time conducting ground-level resupply, a UH-1D has just left materials for Company A, 1st Battalion, 7th Cavalry, during Operation Pershing, late in May 1967. *National Archives*

One job for which Bell UH-1 helicopters were well suited was in the conduct of psychological operations or "psyops," as the military and intelligence agencies sought to influence the thinking of the Vietnamese population. Here, in June 1967, crewmen toss pamphlets out of the door of their UH-1D.
National Archives

The nine UH-1 Hueys seen here, which serve with the 335th Assault Helicopter Company, are airlifting the 4th Battalion, 503rd Infantry, to a site 20 kilometers northwest of Tuy Hòa, where they will launch the search-and-destroy mission Operation Bolling on September 17, 1967. *National Archives*

After conducting a search-and-destroy operation about 5 kilometers southwest of Landing Zone Uplift, South Vietnam, in late October 1967, these infantrymen are being picked up by a mix of UH-1D and UH-1H helicopters of Company A, 2nd Battalion, 8th Cavalry, 1st Air Cavalry Division. *National Archives*

Two UH-1D Hueys, one with "644" stenciled on its tail fin, drop off troops in an open area in Vietnam in October 1967. The utility door, located to the front of the Huey's sliding door, could easily be taken off UH-1Ds and UH-1Hs and has been detached here. *National Archives*

Members of the 56th Transportation Company's Recovery Section from Tân Sơn Nhứt Air Base have
arrived to prepare a UH-1C for transport from this rice paddy to a repair facility. The Huey, seen here on
October 19, 1967, had been shot down near Tân An, in the Mekong delta, southwest of Saigon.
National Archives

In October 1967, a UH-1D Huey hovers near one of the helicopter landing platforms that were developed to facilitate helicopter transport in the swampy Mekong delta of southern Vietnam. Made from aluminum tubing, the platforms had a chain-link surface, were 22 feet in diameter, weighed 900 pounds, and could be airlifted to a desired landing zone by helicopter. These platforms were also designed to function as command posts or first-aid stations. *National Archives*

Resting on its helipad, this UH-1D of the 9th Infantry Division is virtually surrounded by water near Tân An in the Mekong delta, southwest of Saigon, on October 26, 1967. The truck-mounted 1,500-gallon-per-hour ERDLator water purification unit seen in the background was used to make drinkable water from such local water sources as the pools seen here surrounding the helicopter. *National Archives*

Over the Mekong delta in November 1967, a crewman aboard a US Navy UH-1B opens up on Việt Cộng forces with a twin Browning M1919 .30-caliber machine gun. The weapon had recently been installed in the lead chopper of Helicopter Attack (Light) Squadron 3. *National Museum of Naval Aviation*

Maintenance crewmen of Helicopter Attack Squadron (Light) 3 "Seawolves" service two Huey helicopters on November 15, 1967. "Detachment 1" is inscribed on the nose of the chopper on the right. Both Hueys were taking part in Operation Game Warden in southern Vietnam's Mekong delta. *National Museum of Naval Aviation*

As a part of Operation Game Warden—an interdiction operation against the Việt Cộng on Mekong delta waterways—two US Navy Huey helicopters patrol the skies on November 15, 1967. The instrument panel can be seen inside the helicopter in the foreground, while the Huey in the background displays the number "033." *National Museum of Naval Aviation*

In mid-November 1967 a UH-1D airlifts empty water cans from Hill 742 as Companies B and C, 1 Battalion, 8th Infantry, 1st Brigade 4th Infantry Division, prepare to leave the hill, which was about 5 miles northwest of Đắk Tô. *National Archives*

A US Navy armored troop carrier in Vietnam's Mekong delta is the precarious platform on which this Navy UH-1H has landed. The troop carrier was a part of River Assault Flotilla 1 in 1967 when this image was captured. The number "86" is visible on the tail fin of the UH-1H Huey nicknamed "Slick."
National Archives

US soldiers get ready to pour out of a UH-1H helicopter of Troop C, 7th Squadron, 1st Cavalry Regiment (Airmobile), 1st Aviation Brigade, near Tân An, Long An Province, in South Vietnam's Mekong delta, on April 14, 1968. The Huey features yellow markings on its nose and roof. *National Archives*

At Fire Base Berchtesgaden, troops load cases of C rations and ginger ale aboard a UH-1H (with a noteworthy pitot tube atop its roof) during Operation Somerset Plain in early August 1968. Both the sliding and the auxiliary door have been removed, and an M60D machine gun on an M23 mount has been installed in the helicopter. *National Archives*

Crewmen of Detachment 1 (Det-1), Helicopter Attack (Light) Squadron 3 (HAL-3) "Seawolves," make repairs and do maintenance on the engine and rotor assemblies of a UH-1B in about May 1968. Emblazoned on the Huey's nose are the words "DET-1" written in a pseudo-Asian style and, underneath, the HAL-3 emblem, consisting of a standing wolf wielding a trident and holding a shield on which a black ace of spades is displayed. *National Museum of Naval Aviation*

Assigned to Detachment 3, Helicopter Attack (Light) Squadron 3, this UH-1B gunship fires a 2.75-inch FFAR at Việt Cộng forces battling US Navy river patrol boats (PBRs) on the Cổ Chiên River in the Mekong delta in about May 1968.
National Museum of Naval Aviation

Armed with seven-shot rocket pods fitted on atypical tubular pylons, this Marine Corps UH-1E is seen here backing out of a parking revetment at the Marble Mountain Air Facility in Đà Nẵng, Republic of Vietnam, on September 28, 1968. The Huey was assigned to Marine Aircraft Group 16 (MAG-16).
National Museum of Naval Aviation

This US Marine Corps UH-1E ran out of fuel and crashed, landing upside down just south of the Naval Support Activity (NSA) Station Hospital in Đà Nẵng, Quảng Nam Province, South Vietnam, in 1968. Although the crash claimed no lives, four occupants aboard the Huey were injured. *National Museum of Naval Aviation*

A US Navy UH-1B prepares to set down on USS *Garrett County* (LST-786), where another has already been parked. *Garrett County* served as a mobile support base for Navy helicopters and patrol boats as they undertook missions to interdict Việt Cộng activities on Mekong delta waterways. *National Museum of Naval Aviation*

A UH-1H helicopter has just delivered supplies near Landing Zone Buff in the Republic of Vietnam on April 7, 1969. Here, the crew of an Americal Division M113 armored personnel carrier are transferring those supplies into their vehicle. The Huey displays two light-colored bands on its tail boom. *National Archives*

First Lieutenant Jack Hogan is in command of this UH-1E from Marine Light Helicopter Squadron 167 (HML-167) as it prepares to unleash a barrage of 2.75-inch rockets at a concentration of enemy forces south of Đà Nẵng, Republic of Vietnam, on April 9, 1969. *National Museum of Naval Aviation*

With its detached tail boom sitting in a plywood cradle on the roof, a disassembled UH-1D, serial number 66-0971, is pulled by tractor from the hold of a C-124 Globemaster in late July 1969. The Huey will be reassembled at the 520th Aircraft Processing Plant at Tân Sơn Nhứt Air Force Base, Saigon.

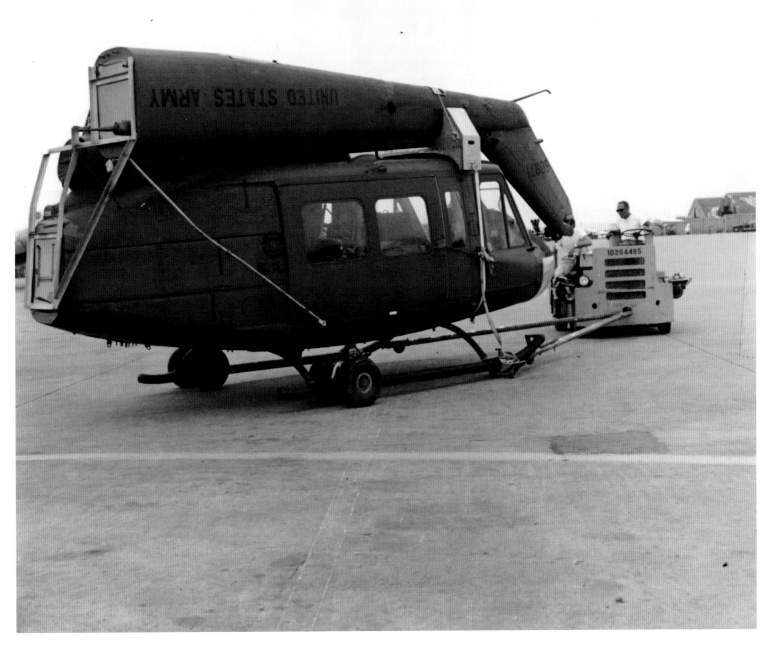

A follow-on photo from the previous image reveals the tractor extracting UH-1D, serial number 66-0971, from the C-124 cargo plane that brought it to Vietnam. The Huey is on its way to the 520th Aircraft Processing Plant at Tân Sơn Nhứt, where it will be reassembled and prepared for service. *National Archives*

Its ground-handling wheels installed on its landing skids, UH-1D 66-0971 has been positioned by a tractor in a revetment at Tân Sơn Nhứt Airbase in July 1969. On the right and in the background are Hueys that have already been assembled. *National Archives*

Now parked in a revetment at Tân Sơn Nhứt Airbase, UH-1D, serial number 66-0971, awaits reassembly in late July 1969. Attached to the tail boom and the rear of the cabin is a bracket made from angle irons. This device secured the tail boom during shipment. *National Archives*

To deprive the enemy of the cover of South Vietnam's lush vegetation, defoliants were sprayed in targeted areas, in what has since become one of the most controversial tactics of the conflict. Huey helicopters were among the aircraft employed for this purpose. Here a UH-1D or -H, serving with the 336th Aviation Company, targets a strip of jungle in the Mekong delta with defoliant on July 26, 1969. *National Archives*

Hovering over the Cửa Lớn River, a US Navy UH-1 backs up a US Navy Patrol Craft, Fast, more commonly known as a Swift Boat, in July 1969. The Huey is armed with the XM16 quad machine gun system and M58 seven-tube 2.75-inch folding-fin aerial rockets or FFARs. Navy patrol boats and helicopters worked together to search out Việt Cộng and their supporters and eliminate them from South Vietnam's coastal waterways. *National Museum of Naval Aviation*

Fitted out with the Fire Fly spotlights system, this Army UH-1D helicopter in Vietnam in August 1969 can illuminate possible targets in the nighttime. Bolted to the floor of this Huey's cargo compartment on a heavy-duty bracket is a Browning M2 .50-caliber machine gun. *National Archives*

Armed with an M60D 7.62mm machine gun on an M23 mount, this UH-1H is assigned to the 11th Combat Aviation Battalion commander in Vietnam in September 1969. Also seen here are the machine gun's ammunition box and flexible ammunition chute. *National Archives*

During a sweep of a region south of the Demilitarized Zone (DMZ) between North and South Vietnam on October 16, 1969, a UH-1H Huey inserts 101st Airborne Division troops into a small open area. Visible on both of the helicopter's sides are the M60D 7.62 mm machine guns of the M23 Helicopter Subarmament System. In the lowered position under the Huey's nose is the landing light. *National Archives*

This UH-1H medevac helicopter rescues a wounded soldier near the DMZ in Vietnam on October 16, 1969. Pioneers in medical evacuation or "medevac" as it evolved over the course of the Vietnam War, the 57th Medical Detachment (Helicopter Ambulance) used the call sign "Dust Off," which eventually became synonymous with medevac and helicopter rescue missions. As the war continued, other units carried on the 57th's tradition. *National Archives*

Armed with M60D machine guns in its doors, a UH-1H helicopter hovers over the area of Long Bình, South Vietnam, on October 6, 1969. On the ground below the aircraft, members of Company C, 2nd Battalion, 3rd Infantry, 199th Light Infantry Brigade, together with crewmen of an M113 Armored Cavalry Assault Vehicle (ACAV), have taken up a defensive posture. *National Archives*

As a US Army UH-1H passes overhead—a crewman manning its M60D machine gun—and covered by an M113 ACAV, the same unit seen in the previous image now prepares to move out near Long Bình on October 6, 1969. *National Archives*

The insignia of the US Army's 1st Signal Brigade is emblazoned on the nose of the second UH-1H in this line of Hueys drawn up at Nha Trang Airbase, Republic of Vietnam, in November 1969. These helicopters ferried Signal personnel and materiel throughout the Central Vietnam Highlands, the part of the country designated as II Corps Area. *National Archives*

A UH-1H transports a cargo of steel cables to 47th Infantry Regiment troops in May 1970, during the US incursion into Cambodia. Visible at the scene are a number of M113 personnel carriers, including one ACAV. *National Archives*

A gunner mans the M60 machine gun in the open cargo door of a UH-1B Huey, conducting a patrol of South Vietnam's waterways on June 29, 1970. Visible on the aircraft's nose is the insignia of the Helicopter Attack Squadron (Light) 3 "Seawolves." *National Museum of Naval Aviation*

Personnel from Company E, 4th Battalion, 21st Infantry, offload a treasured haul of cola and beer from a Huey. Beer and soft drinks, such as those being delivered here at Landing Zone Charlie Brown, southeast of Đức Phổ in Quảng Ngãi Province, on July 9, 1970, were highly prized morale boosters in the South Vietnamese summer heat. *National Archives*

In addition to US forces, the Royal Australian Air Force (RAAF) also flew Huey helicopters in Vietnam. A door gunner aboard an RAAF UH-1H of No. 9 Squadron makes eye contact with a photographer on the ground as his Huey sets down at the foot of the Núi Thị Vải hills complex in Phước Tuy Province, southeast of Saigon, on July 20, 1970. *National Archives*

An RAAF UH-1D of No. 9 Squadron takes on troops of Company B, 2nd Royal Australian Army Regiment, along the foot of the Núi Thị Vải hills complex, southeast of Saigon, Republic of Vietnam, on July 20, 1970. *National Archives*

A flight crewman is at the M60D 7.62 mm machine gun as his UH-1H of No. 9 Squadron, RAAF—probably the same aircraft as appears in the previous photograph—lifts off from a site near the Núi Thị Vài hills on July 20, 1970. *National Archives*

Having cleared the ground, this UH-1H of No. 9 Squadron, RAAF, moves forward during a July 20, 1970, mission in the Republic of Vietnam. Painted on the tail fin is red, white, and dark-blue Australian fin flash, and marked on the tail boom are the letters "RAAF." *National Archives*

Two 2nd Royal Australian Regiment soldiers load boxes of rations onto a UH-1H Huey assigned to the RAAF's No. 9 Squadron. The goods are to be transported to the 2nd Battalion Australian and New Zealand Army Corps (ANZAC) in their base at Núi Đất, Phước Tuy Province, southeast of Saigon, on July 21, 1970. *National Archives*

Soldiers of the 2nd ANZAC Battalion pass along rations and other supplies to be loaded into the cargo compartment of an RAAF UH-1H at Núi Đất on July 21, 1970. Bell UH-1D helicopters were also flown by the RAAF during the Vietnam War. *National Archives*

The emblem of a white duck head over a blue crown that is emblazoned on the pilot's door of this RAAF helicopter is the insignia of No. 9 Squadron. Aboard this Huey at Núi Đất, southeast of Saigon, on July 22, 1970, an aircrewman is removing the bullet trap safety device from a Minigun. *National Archives*

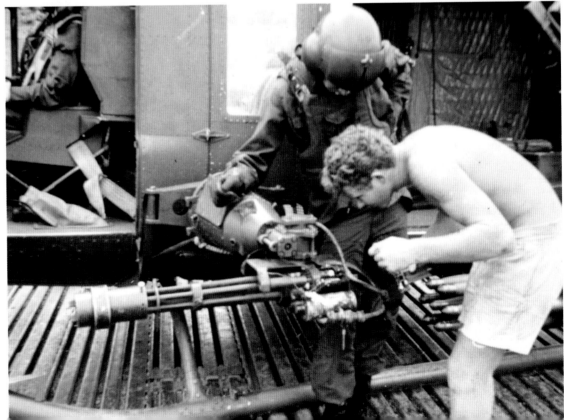

Dressed for the tropical July heat of southern Vietnam, this maintenance technician of No. 9 Squadron of the RAAF is troubleshooting a 7.62 mm Minigun that had jammed during a recent operation. The pilot occupies an armored seat. The Australians referred to their armed Hueys as Bushrangers. *National Archives*

Four 7.62 mm ammunition boxes were needed to supply ammo to the two General Electric M134 Miniguns as they were mounted on Huey helicopters. With a rate of fire of 2,000 or 4,000 rounds per minute per gun, the Miniguns could expend a lot of ammunition is a very short amount of time. A member of the RAAF's No. 9 Squadron is here loading 7.62 mm ammunition into the ammo boxes at the Australian base at Núi Đất on July 22, 1970. *National Archives*

Members of the 162nd Aviation Company (Combat Assault) remove an M134 Minigun's mount from a Huey at Cần Thơ, largest city in the Mekong delta, southwest of Saigon, in July 1970. To the left, one crewman holds the gun mount and adapter. An unshrouded, seven-tube 2.75-inch FFAR launcher can be seen below the mount. This type of launcher was superior to the podded FFAR launcher inasmuch as it could more easily be repaired if one or more of the tubes were damaged or inoperative. *National Archives*

Two members of No. 9 Squadron of the RAAF load 2.75-inch FFARs into a 2.75-inch M158 rocket pod at the squadron's base in the Republic of Vietnam. A twin M60 7.62 mm machine gun can be seen mounted on a pedestal fixed to the pylon for external stores.
National Archives

This member of an air crew from No. 9 Squadron is getting ready to set off on a mission. As has already been seen in previous photos, the Australians were known to install two external-stores pylons on each side of their UH-1D and UH-1H gunships. A Minigun would be mounted on one of those pylons, while rockets would be fitted on the other.
National Archives

Assigned to the 11th Combat Aviation Group at Phú Lợi, Bình Dương Province, north of Saigon, in September 1970, this UH-1M (i.e., a UH-1C upgraded with the installation of a T53-L-13 engine) has been fitted with the Hughes INFANT (Iroquois Night Fighter and Night Tracker), with an infrared video camera and image-intensifier scope.
National Archives

With the XM93 armament system, door mounts for two M134 7.62 mm Miniguns were installed in long-fuselage Huey helicopters. The Minigun was fitted on a flexible mount, with a pair of handgrips. A flexible hose to channel ejected spent casings was connected to a collector tray located below the gun cradle.
National Archives

Parked on the flight line at the Army airfield in Cần Thơ, southwest of Saigon in South Vietnam's Mekong delta, is a UH-1C assigned to the 162nd Aviation Company (Combat Assault). Seen here in 1970, the Huey is equipped with the M21 armament subsystem, which includes a pair of M158 2.75-inch FFAR launchers and two Miniguns. White position lights extend from the sides of the rear of the tail boom. Positioning the white taillights on the rear of the tail boom is a distinct feature of the C-model Huey. Other UH-1 helicopters had those lights on the trailing edge of the fin. The right-angle final-drive gearbox (plus the shaft) and also the tail rotor were located at the top of the tail fin. *National Archives*

At the Cần Thơ Army Airfield in the Mekong delta in 1970, a crew chief puts grease on a Huey's rotor head. The aircraft was serving with the 162nd Aviation Company (Combat Assault). The Huey's transmission is below the rotor head, while the rotor hub is visible above the crew chief's head. The Huey was a comparatively small helicopter, but despite this it was packed with a hodgepodge of control linkages, electrical and hydraulic lines, and complex mechanisms. *National Archives*

The engine and transmission fairings are removed for maintenance from this short-fuselage UH-1C from the 162nd Aviation Company (Combat Assault) at Cần Thơ in 1970. The engine fairing was split at the top fore and aft, with each section hinged at the rear. This UH-1C is identifiable by the Bell 540 "door hinge" high-speed rotor. The rotor blades droop equally on each side of the rotor head, since the rotor head plate bends at the mast. Other Hueys have blades that angle up a few degrees from each other in their semirigid rotor heads. *National Archives*

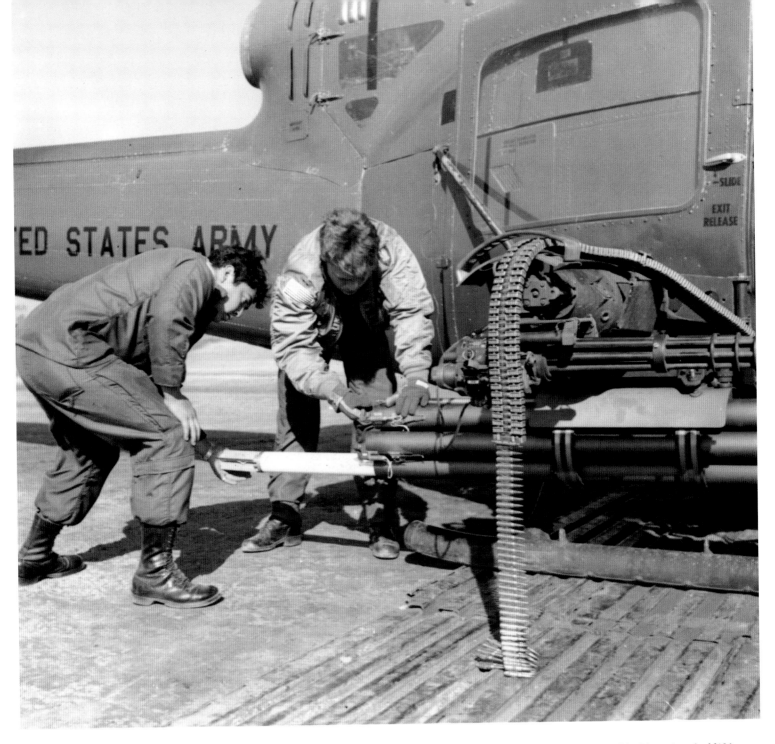

Aboard a short-fuselage Huey, two soldiers load 2.75-inch FFARs into their M158 launcher. An M134 7.62 mm Minigun and the flex chute for its ammunition are visible above the launcher. Belted 7.62 mm ammunition hangs from the flex chute's bottom. *National Archives*

Transporting troops of the 502nd Infantry, these three UH-1 Hueys, serving with the 101st Assault Helicopter Battalion, 101st Airborne Division (Airmobile), are preparing to set down at a fire-support base located southwest of Huế, in the northern part of the Republic of Vietnam, during 1970. *National Archives*

On a mission to pick up and extract a team of soldiers from Company C, 1st Battalion, 327th Airborne Infantry, 101st Airborne Division, a Huey has set down in a small open area in South Vietnam on April 15, 1971. The Huey will return the men to Fire Support Base Birmingham, some 7 miles southwest of Huế. *National Archives*

The UH-1P was used by the "Green Hornets," the US Air Force 20th Special Operations Squadron in Vietnam. Serial number 65-7929 (*foreground*) and 63-13162, both armed with a pair of Miniguns, are on a mission. Each of the weapons is capable of unleashing a fusillade of 4,000 7.62 mm rounds per minute per gun, giving this formation considerable firepower. The helicopter in the foreground is further armed with a pair of seven-tube 2.75 rocket launchers. *Capt. Billie Dee Tedford, via National Museum of the United States Air Force*

Here seen hauling lumber, this UH-1P serves with the 20th Special Operations Squadron at Đức Lập camp in the Republic of Vietnam's Central Highlands, just 14 kilometers from the Cambodian border. Part of the 20th SOS's cobra symbol can be seen to the left on the tail boom. The T58-GE-3 engine's sideward-pointing exhaust is also visible. *DVIC*

This Green Hornets UH-1P crew, their helicopter armed and ready, await orders to depart on a covert mission. The crewman in the rear cargo door is resting his legs on a flexible ladder that could be extended to pick up personnel when the helicopter could not land. *US Air Force photo*

Refueling for a mission at Đắk Tô, Republic of Vietnam, are two helicopters serving with the 20th Special Operations Squadron's "Green Hornets." The UH-1P in the foreground, serial number 65-7931, displays the right-facing engine exhaust nozzle that was a distinctive feature of the UH-1F model, from which the UH-1Ps were converted. *Army Aviation Museum*

A crewman occupies the doorway of a UH-1P helicopter. Used in a special-operations role, the UH-1P is unmarked and features twin blade antennas on the roof of the cabin and has its exhaust routed through the right side of the engine fairing. *Capt. Billie Dee Tedford, via National Museum of the United States Air Force*

This UH-1P Huey in Southeast Asia camouflage, with the number "162" stenciled in black on its nose, belongs to the South Vietnamese air force. On the external-stores mount is a seven-shot 2.75-inch FFAR pod. A Sikorsky H-34 Choctaw helicopter—also lacking visible markings—is visible in the background. *Capt. Billie Dee Tedford, via National Museum of the United States Air Force*

At a base in Vietnam, an apparently unmarked US Air Force UH-1P with two blade antennas is receiving a new engine. Over the course of the war in Vietnam, about twenty USAF UH-1F helicopters were converted into UH-1Ps for exclusive use in special operations and on psychological-warfare missions. The only user of the UH-1P helicopter in Vietnam was the 20th Special Operations Squadron.
Capt. Billie Dee Tedford, via National Museum of the United States Air Force